PRINCEWILL LAGANG

The Psychology of Entrepreneurship: Understanding the Mind of Success

First published by PRINCEWILL LAGANG 2023

Copyright © 2023 by Princewill Lagang

All rights reserved. No part of this publication may be reproduced, stored or transmitted in any form or by any means, electronic, mechanical, photocopying, recording, scanning, or otherwise without written permission from the publisher. It is illegal to copy this book, post it to a website, or distribute it by any other means without permission.

Princewill Lagang asserts the moral right to be identified as the author of this work.

First edition

This book was professionally typeset on Reedsy.
Find out more at reedsy.com

Contents

1. The Psychology of Entrepreneurship — 1
2. The Entrepreneurial Journey: From Idea to Action — 5
3. Business Development and Growth: Navigating the... — 9
4. Entrepreneurial Decision-Making: Navigating Uncertainty and... — 13
5. Resilience: The Entrepreneur's Secret Weapon — 16
6. Creativity and Innovation: The Entrepreneur's Competitive... — 19
7. Ethics and Social Responsibility in Entrepreneurship — 23
8. Technology and Entrepreneurship: Navigating the Digital... — 27
9. Entrepreneurial Leadership: Guiding Vision to Reality — 31
10. Thriving in Entrepreneurship: A Roadmap to Success — 35
11. Summary — 39
12. Chapter 12 — 42

1

The Psychology of Entrepreneurship

Title: Understanding the Mind of Success

Introduction

Entrepreneurship is often celebrated for its potential to create wealth, drive innovation, and transform economies. It's a world where visionaries and risk-takers thrive, where the lines between work and passion blur, and where the status quo is challenged and reshaped. Yet, behind every successful entrepreneur is a complex interplay of thoughts, emotions, and behaviors that define their journey. This book, "The Psychology of Entrepreneurship: Understanding the Mind of Success," delves deep into the intricacies of the entrepreneurial mind, aiming to uncover the underlying factors that lead to success in this challenging domain.

Entrepreneurship is not just about starting a business; it's about creating, leading, and sustaining a venture through its ups and downs. It's about identifying opportunities in the midst of uncertainty, making bold decisions, and managing the inevitable risks. To understand the psychology of entrepreneurship, we must explore the thoughts and feelings that drive individuals to take these risks, persevere through adversity, and ultimately thrive.

In this first chapter, we will set the stage for our exploration into the minds of successful entrepreneurs. We will discuss the basic concepts of psychology and entrepreneurship, why understanding the psychology of entrepreneurs is essential, and what you can expect to learn from this book. We will explore the unique mindset and characteristics that often set entrepreneurs apart, and why they are critical for success in this field.

Understanding the Psychology of Entrepreneurs

Entrepreneurship is a dynamic field that requires a combination of technical skills, business acumen, and personal qualities that make individuals thrive in the face of uncertainty. While business skills can be learned and developed, the underlying psychological traits and tendencies that drive entrepreneurial success are often deeply ingrained.

The psychology of entrepreneurs is a multidimensional concept that encompasses various aspects of an individual's mental and emotional makeup. These aspects include their:

1. Motivation: What drives someone to become an entrepreneur? Is it a desire for financial independence, the pursuit of a passion, or a need to solve a specific problem? Understanding an entrepreneur's motivation is crucial to comprehending their behavior and decision-making.

2. Risk Tolerance: Entrepreneurs often take risks that others might avoid. Their ability to tolerate and even embrace risk is a significant factor in their success. We will delve into the psychology behind risk-taking and how it affects the entrepreneurial journey.

3. Resilience: The road to entrepreneurial success is rarely smooth. Failure and setbacks are common. Resilience is the ability to bounce back from

adversity, and it plays a vital role in the life of an entrepreneur.

4. Creativity and Innovation: Entrepreneurship thrives on creativity and the ability to innovate. We will explore the cognitive processes that drive creative thinking and how entrepreneurs harness their creativity to develop unique solutions and products.

5. Decision-Making: Entrepreneurial decision-making is often complex and involves assessing various factors. We will examine the cognitive biases that can influence an entrepreneur's choices and how they can make more informed decisions.

Why Study the Psychology of Entrepreneurship?

Understanding the psychology of entrepreneurship offers several benefits. First, it can provide insights for aspiring entrepreneurs looking to navigate the challenges of starting and running a business. Secondly, it can offer established entrepreneurs tools to enhance their decision-making, leadership, and overall success. Finally, policymakers and educators can use this knowledge to foster entrepreneurial ecosystems that nurture and support individuals with these unique psychological traits.

What to Expect from This Book

In the chapters that follow, we will delve into each aspect of the psychology of entrepreneurship, providing real-life examples, research findings, and practical insights. We will explore the experiences and journeys of successful entrepreneurs, shedding light on how their psychology has played a pivotal role in their achievements.

Throughout the book, you will find exercises, case studies, and actionable advice that will help you develop and apply the principles of entrepreneurial psychology in your own life. Whether you're an aspiring entrepreneur, an established business owner, an educator, or a policymaker, this book aims to offer a comprehensive understanding of the psychology of entrepreneurship and how it contributes to the creation of successful businesses.

As we embark on this journey into the minds of successful entrepreneurs, keep in mind that the path to success is as unique as the individuals who walk it. The journey may be filled with challenges, but understanding the psychology of entrepreneurship can be a guiding light, helping you unlock your full potential and embrace the world of possibilities that entrepreneurship offers.

2

The Entrepreneurial Journey: From Idea to Action

Introduction

In the previous chapter, we laid the groundwork for understanding the psychology of entrepreneurship and the unique mindset of successful entrepreneurs. Now, in Chapter 2, we will embark on a journey through the entrepreneurial process, exploring how ideas are transformed into viable businesses. This chapter is all about taking those first steps, from the initial spark of inspiration to the critical action that sets the entrepreneurial endeavor in motion.

The entrepreneurial journey is often romanticized, but it is far from a linear path. It's a process filled with twists, turns, and challenges that test an entrepreneur's mettle. We will dive into the psychological factors that underpin each stage of this journey, shedding light on the thought processes and emotional dynamics that drive entrepreneurs forward.

From Idea to Opportunity

THE PSYCHOLOGY OF ENTREPRENEURSHIP: UNDERSTANDING THE MIND OF SUCCESS

1. Inspiration Strikes: The entrepreneurial journey often begins with a moment of inspiration. Entrepreneurs notice a problem that needs solving or identify an unmet need. This chapter will explore the psychological aspects of recognizing and framing these opportunities, examining how creativity and problem-solving play a vital role.

2. Passion and Motivation: Successful entrepreneurs are often deeply passionate about their ideas. We'll discuss the role of passion in fueling motivation and the psychological factors that help entrepreneurs stay committed to their vision.

3. Idea Validation: Before fully committing to an idea, entrepreneurs must validate its feasibility. We'll explore how entrepreneurs use critical thinking and market research to assess the potential of their ideas.

The Decision to Act

1. Overcoming Fear and Doubt: Fear of failure and self-doubt are common psychological barriers that can paralyze potential entrepreneurs. We'll delve into the strategies and mindset shifts that help individuals overcome these challenges.

2. Risk Perception: The decision to act often involves assessing and managing risks. We'll examine how entrepreneurs perceive and approach risk, including the cognitive biases that can affect their risk assessment.

3. Goal Setting and Planning: Entrepreneurs are goal-oriented individuals. We'll discuss the psychological aspects of setting clear goals, creating plans, and staying organized, which are crucial for moving from idea to action.

Taking the Leap

1. Proactive Behavior: The transition from idea to action requires taking

the leap, making that first move. We will explore the psychological traits that enable proactive behavior and the impact of decisiveness on the entrepreneurial journey.

2. Perseverance: The initial steps are often fraught with challenges. We'll discuss the role of resilience and perseverance in helping entrepreneurs navigate setbacks and continue moving forward.

3. Adaptability: Entrepreneurs must adapt to changing circumstances. We'll examine the psychological factors that enable individuals to pivot, adjust their strategies, and stay agile in the face of uncertainty.

Case Studies and Real-Life Experiences

Throughout this chapter, we will draw from the experiences of successful entrepreneurs to illustrate the psychological principles discussed. These real-life case studies will provide concrete examples of how individuals have navigated the early stages of the entrepreneurial journey, offering insights and inspiration.

Practical Exercises

To help you apply the concepts discussed in this chapter, you will find practical exercises and activities that encourage you to reflect on your own entrepreneurial ideas and take the first steps toward turning them into reality. These exercises are designed to help you develop the psychological skills and mindset needed for entrepreneurial success.

Conclusion

Chapter 2 takes us on the journey from idea to action, providing a comprehensive understanding of the psychological factors that drive entrepreneurs to take those crucial first steps. By the end of this chapter, you will have a deeper appreciation for the challenges and opportunities that arise in the early stages of entrepreneurship and the mindset required to overcome them. The next chapter will continue our exploration of the entrepreneurial journey, focusing on the critical phase of business development and growth.

3

Business Development and Growth: Navigating the Entrepreneurial Landscape

Introduction

In Chapter 2, we explored the initial stages of the entrepreneurial journey, from the birth of an idea to the courageous leap into action. Now, in Chapter 3, we move forward to the pivotal phase of business development and growth. This chapter delves into the psychological dynamics that drive entrepreneurs to build and expand their ventures, transform them into sustainable businesses, and ultimately achieve success.

Business development and growth are complex and multifaceted processes that require a unique set of skills, strategies, and, most importantly, a particular mindset. Entrepreneurs in this phase must deal with challenges such as scaling operations, securing funding, and competing in the marketplace. To succeed, they must navigate these challenges while maintaining their vision, motivation, and adaptability.

In this chapter, we will explore the psychological underpinnings of business development and growth, covering various aspects that are essential for entrepreneurial success.

Vision and Strategy

1. Clarifying the Vision: Entrepreneurs often need to revisit and refine their vision as their businesses grow. We'll explore the psychological aspects of maintaining a clear and compelling vision and how it drives decision-making.

2. Strategic Thinking: Developing a well-defined strategy is crucial for growth. We'll discuss how entrepreneurs use strategic thinking to set goals, make informed decisions, and allocate resources effectively.

3. Innovation and Adaptation: To stay competitive, entrepreneurs must continually innovate and adapt. We'll explore the psychology of innovation and how entrepreneurs foster a culture of creativity within their organizations.

Leadership and Team Building

1. Leadership Styles: Entrepreneurial leaders play a pivotal role in shaping the culture and direction of their businesses. We'll examine different leadership styles and their psychological foundations.

2. Team Building and Motivation: As businesses expand, building and motivating a high-performing team becomes essential. We'll discuss how entrepreneurs leverage psychological principles to create a cohesive and motivated workforce.

Funding and Financial Management

1. Raising Capital: Securing funding is often a critical challenge in the growth phase. We'll explore the psychology of fundraising, including pitch strategies and managing the emotional aspects of seeking investment.

2. Financial Decision-Making: Effective financial management is key to growth. We'll examine how entrepreneurs make sound financial decisions and manage resources wisely.

Market Expansion and Competition

1. Market Entry Strategies: Expanding into new markets is a significant growth opportunity. We'll discuss the psychological aspects of market analysis, entry strategies, and the importance of understanding local consumer behavior.

2. Competitive Advantage: Entrepreneurs must continually differentiate themselves in competitive markets. We'll explore the psychology behind building and maintaining a sustainable competitive advantage.

Case Studies and Real-Life Experiences

Throughout this chapter, we will draw on the experiences of successful entrepreneurs who have navigated the challenges of business development and growth. These real-life examples will provide practical insights and illustrate the psychological principles discussed.

Practical Exercises

To help you apply the concepts explored in this chapter, practical exercises and activities are included. These exercises are designed to guide you in developing the psychological skills and mindset needed to effectively manage the growth of your entrepreneurial venture.

Conclusion

Chapter 3 takes us through the critical phase of business development and growth, where entrepreneurs transform their ideas into sustainable businesses. By understanding the psychological factors that drive this phase of the entrepreneurial journey, you will be better equipped to overcome challenges and seize opportunities as your venture evolves. In the next chapter, we will explore the dynamic world of entrepreneurial decision-making, examining the intricate processes that guide entrepreneurs through complex choices and uncertainties.

4

Entrepreneurial Decision-Making: Navigating Uncertainty and Complexity

Introduction

In the earlier chapters, we journeyed through the inception of entrepreneurial ideas, the courageous leap into action, and the challenges of business development and growth. Now, in Chapter 4, we delve into the heart of the entrepreneurial process – decision-making. The decisions entrepreneurs make at every juncture can shape the course of their ventures, from strategic choices to everyday operational decisions.

Entrepreneurial decision-making is a complex interplay of cognitive processes, emotional responses, and external factors. Entrepreneurs often find themselves navigating uncertainty, taking calculated risks, and adapting to rapidly changing environments. This chapter explores the psychological dynamics that underpin entrepreneurial decision-making, providing insights into how successful entrepreneurs approach, evaluate, and make choices in the face of uncertainty and complexity.

The Complexity of Entrepreneurial Decision-Making

1. Cognitive Biases: We'll start by examining common cognitive biases that can influence decision-making, such as confirmation bias, overconfidence, and anchoring, and how entrepreneurs can mitigate their effects.

2. Emotions and Decision-Making: Emotions play a significant role in entrepreneurial decision-making. We'll explore the emotional rollercoaster that entrepreneurs often experience and how to harness these emotions for better decision-making.

Strategic Decision-Making

1. Strategic Thinking: Entrepreneurs must make high-stakes strategic decisions that can impact the long-term success of their ventures. We'll delve into how they engage in strategic thinking and prioritize their options.

2. Risk Assessment: Assessing and managing risk is a critical aspect of strategic decision-making. We'll discuss how entrepreneurs weigh the pros and cons, make risk-aware choices, and cope with the fear of failure.

Operational Decision-Making

1. Operational Efficiency: Day-to-day decisions impact the efficiency and effectiveness of a business. We'll explore how entrepreneurs maintain operational efficiency through decision-making.

2. Adaptability: The entrepreneurial landscape is dynamic. Entrepreneurs must be adaptable and responsive to change. We'll discuss how the psychology of adaptability influences daily decision-making.

Collaborative Decision-Making

1. Team Dynamics: As ventures grow, decision-making often involves collaboration with a team. We'll explore the psychological dynamics of team

decision-making and how entrepreneurs build a decision-making culture.

2. Delegation: Entrepreneurs must delegate decisions as their ventures expand. We'll discuss the psychology of effective delegation and trust in decision-makers.

Case Studies and Real-Life Experiences

Throughout this chapter, we will draw on real-life experiences of successful entrepreneurs who have faced complex and uncertain decisions. These case studies will illustrate the psychological principles discussed and provide practical examples of how entrepreneurs approach various decision-making scenarios.

Practical Exercises

To help you apply the concepts explored in this chapter, practical exercises and decision-making scenarios are included. These exercises are designed to help you develop the psychological skills and mindset needed to make effective decisions in your own entrepreneurial endeavors.

Conclusion

Chapter 4 sheds light on the intricate processes of entrepreneurial decision-making. Understanding the psychological factors that influence choices in the entrepreneurial context is essential for success, as it enables entrepreneurs to make informed, rational decisions while navigating the inherent uncertainties and complexities of their ventures. In the next chapter, we will explore the critical role of resilience in the entrepreneurial journey, as entrepreneurs face setbacks and challenges on their path to success.

5

Resilience: The Entrepreneur's Secret Weapon

Introduction

The entrepreneurial journey is a path fraught with challenges, setbacks, and moments of uncertainty. In Chapter 5, we explore the critical role of resilience in the life of an entrepreneur. Resilience is the ability to bounce back from adversity, to persevere through tough times, and to thrive in the face of uncertainty. It is often described as the entrepreneur's secret weapon, as it empowers individuals to weather the storms of business and emerge stronger on the other side.

This chapter delves into the psychological dimensions of resilience, providing insights into how successful entrepreneurs develop and maintain this invaluable trait. Resilience is not an innate quality but a skill that can be cultivated, and understanding the psychological foundations of resilience is essential for entrepreneurs seeking to thrive in the ever-changing landscape of business.

RESILIENCE: THE ENTREPRENEUR'S SECRET WEAPON

Understanding Resilience

1. The Resilience Mindset: Resilient entrepreneurs possess a specific mindset. We'll explore the psychological characteristics that define this mindset, including adaptability, optimism, and a growth-oriented perspective.

2. Psychological Strategies for Resilience: Entrepreneurs employ various psychological strategies to bolster their resilience. These strategies include reframing challenges as opportunities, maintaining a sense of purpose, and building a support network.

Coping with Failure and Setbacks

1. Managing Failure: Failure is an inherent part of entrepreneurship. We'll discuss how entrepreneurs cope with failure, bounce back from it, and leverage it as a learning opportunity.

2. Handling Setbacks: The entrepreneurial journey is riddled with setbacks, from financial crises to product failures. We'll explore the psychological tactics entrepreneurs use to navigate these challenges and keep moving forward.

Stress Management

1. Stress and Burnout: The entrepreneurial path can be stressful, and burnout is a real risk. We'll delve into the psychological aspects of managing stress, preventing burnout, and promoting mental well-being.

2. Self-Care: Entrepreneurs need to prioritize self-care. We'll discuss how taking care of one's physical and mental health contributes to resilience.

Case Studies and Real-Life Experiences

Throughout this chapter, we will draw on real-life experiences of successful entrepreneurs who have demonstrated exceptional resilience in the face of adversity. These case studies will illustrate the psychological principles discussed and provide practical examples of how resilience has played a pivotal role in their journeys.

Practical Exercises

To help you apply the concepts explored in this chapter, practical exercises and resilience-building activities are included. These exercises are designed to guide you in developing the psychological skills and mindset needed to cultivate resilience in your own entrepreneurial endeavors.

Conclusion

Chapter 5 sheds light on the psychological underpinnings of resilience, a crucial trait that empowers entrepreneurs to face adversity, adapt to change, and thrive in challenging circumstances. By understanding and applying the principles of resilience, entrepreneurs can enhance their ability to overcome setbacks and emerge stronger, better equipped to navigate the entrepreneurial journey. In the next chapter, we will delve into the critical realm of creativity and innovation, exploring how entrepreneurs harness their creative potential to drive business success.

6

Creativity and Innovation: The Entrepreneur's Competitive Edge

Introduction

Creativity and innovation are the lifeblood of entrepreneurship. In Chapter 6, we dive into the dynamic world of entrepreneurial creativity and innovation, exploring how these qualities give entrepreneurs a competitive edge and drive business success. This chapter illuminates the psychological dimensions of creativity and innovation, unveiling the cognitive processes and mindsets that underpin the entrepreneurial ability to generate novel ideas, products, and solutions.

Successful entrepreneurs are not just visionary thinkers; they are also creative problem solvers who challenge the status quo and develop innovative offerings. This chapter provides insights into the psychological factors that fuel entrepreneurial creativity and innovation and offers guidance on how aspiring entrepreneurs can nurture and harness these essential skills.

The Creative Mindset

1. Creativity as a Process: We'll discuss the process of creativity and how it involves idea generation, incubation, and the "eureka" moment. We'll also explore the psychological principles that underlie this process.

2. The Growth Mindset: A growth mindset is pivotal for nurturing creativity. We'll examine how entrepreneurs with a growth mindset view challenges and failures as opportunities for growth.

Idea Generation and Problem-Solving

1. Divergent Thinking: Entrepreneurs excel in divergent thinking, a process that involves generating a wide range of potential solutions to a problem. We'll explore the psychological traits that enable entrepreneurs to think divergently.

2. Problem-Solving Strategies: Successful entrepreneurs employ problem-solving strategies, such as design thinking and reframing, to address complex challenges. We'll delve into these strategies and their psychological foundations.

Innovation in Practice

1. Innovation Culture: Creating a culture of innovation is essential for driving creative ideas to fruition. We'll discuss the psychological dynamics of fostering innovation within an entrepreneurial team or organization.

2. User-Centered Innovation: Understanding and empathizing with the end user is central to innovation. We'll explore how entrepreneurs employ psychological techniques to design products and services that meet real-world needs.

Risk-Taking and Entrepreneurial Innovation

1. Risk-Taking and Innovation: Innovation often involves calculated risk. We'll discuss the relationship between risk-taking and entrepreneurial innovation, and how entrepreneurs manage risk when pushing the boundaries of their industries.

2. Learning from Failure: Failure is an intrinsic part of the innovation process. We'll explore how entrepreneurs leverage failures as stepping stones to innovation and success.

Case Studies and Real-Life Experiences

Throughout this chapter, we will draw on the experiences of successful entrepreneurs who have harnessed creativity and innovation to drive their ventures. These real-life case studies will illustrate the psychological principles discussed and provide practical examples of how entrepreneurs have leveraged creativity and innovation in their entrepreneurial journeys.

Practical Exercises

To help you apply the concepts explored in this chapter, practical exercises and creativity-enhancing activities are included. These exercises are designed to guide you in developing the psychological skills and mindset needed to cultivate creativity and innovation in your own entrepreneurial endeavors.

Conclusion

Chapter 6 illuminates the psychology of entrepreneurial creativity and innovation, uncovering the cognitive processes and mindsets that enable entrepreneurs to generate novel ideas and develop groundbreaking solutions. By understanding and applying the principles of creativity and innovation, entrepreneurs can unlock their potential and stay at the forefront of their industries, continually driving business success. In the next chapter, we will explore the role of ethics and social responsibility in entrepreneurship, emphasizing the importance of building businesses that contribute positively to society.

7

Ethics and Social Responsibility in Entrepreneurship

Introduction

Entrepreneurship is not only about creating wealth and innovation; it also carries a profound responsibility to society and the environment. In Chapter 7, we delve into the critical and often overlooked aspects of ethics and social responsibility in entrepreneurship. This chapter explores the psychological dimensions of ethical decision-making and the strategies that successful entrepreneurs employ to build businesses that contribute positively to society.

In the contemporary entrepreneurial landscape, stakeholders, from consumers to investors, increasingly demand ethical behavior and social responsibility from businesses. Entrepreneurs who understand the psychological foundations of ethical entrepreneurship can create sustainable and socially conscious ventures, fostering trust, reputation, and long-term success.

The Foundations of Ethical Entrepreneurship

1. Ethical Decision-Making: Ethical entrepreneurship begins with ethical decision-making. We'll discuss the psychological principles that guide entrepreneurs in making moral and responsible choices.

2. Moral Values and Beliefs: The personal values and beliefs of entrepreneurs play a significant role in shaping ethical behavior. We'll explore how entrepreneurs develop and maintain a moral compass in the face of complex decisions.

Creating Ethical Ventures

1. Corporate Social Responsibility: Entrepreneurs have a unique opportunity to shape corporate social responsibility (CSR) initiatives. We'll discuss how entrepreneurs develop and implement CSR strategies that align with their values and benefit society.

2. Sustainability: Building sustainable businesses is not only an ethical choice but also an economic imperative. We'll explore the psychological factors that drive entrepreneurs to adopt sustainable practices.

Stakeholder Engagement

1. Customer-Centric Ethics: The relationship between businesses and customers is pivotal. We'll examine how entrepreneurs employ ethical practices, such as transparency and fairness, to build trust and loyalty among customers.

2. Employee Well-Being: Caring for employees is a hallmark of ethical entrepreneurship. We'll discuss how entrepreneurs create work environments that prioritize employee well-being and personal growth.

Ethical Challenges and Dilemmas

1. Navigating Ethical Dilemmas: Entrepreneurs often face complex ethical dilemmas. We'll explore the psychological strategies they use to navigate these dilemmas and make ethically sound decisions.

2. Ethical Leadership: Ethical leadership is critical for fostering a culture of ethics within an organization. We'll discuss the psychological attributes of ethical leaders and their impact on the entire team.

Case Studies and Real-Life Experiences

Throughout this chapter, we will draw on the experiences of successful entrepreneurs who have championed ethical and socially responsible entrepreneurship. These real-life case studies will illustrate the psychological principles discussed and provide practical examples of how entrepreneurs have integrated ethics and social responsibility into their ventures.

Practical Exercises

To help you apply the concepts explored in this chapter, practical exercises and ethical decision-making scenarios are included. These exercises are designed to guide you in developing the psychological skills and mindset needed to embrace ethical entrepreneurship in your own ventures.

Conclusion

Chapter 7 highlights the crucial role of ethics and social responsibility in entrepreneurship, emphasizing the importance of building businesses that make a positive impact on society and the environment. Entrepreneurs who understand the psychological dimensions of ethical entrepreneurship can foster trust, loyalty, and long-term success, creating ventures that are not only profitable but also responsible and sustainable. In the next chapter, we will explore the ever-evolving landscape of technology and its impact on entrepreneurial endeavors, offering insights into how entrepreneurs can leverage technology for success.

8

Technology and Entrepreneurship: Navigating the Digital Frontier

Introduction

In today's fast-paced business world, technology is an integral part of entrepreneurship. In Chapter 8, we delve into the dynamic intersection of technology and entrepreneurship, exploring the psychological dimensions of how entrepreneurs navigate the digital frontier. This chapter provides insights into the mindset and strategies that successful entrepreneurs employ to leverage technology for business success.

The advent of the digital age has transformed the entrepreneurial landscape, presenting both opportunities and challenges. Entrepreneurs who understand the psychological foundations of technology integration can harness its power to enhance efficiency, expand their reach, and drive innovation.

The Digital Mindset

1. Technological Adaptability: Successful entrepreneurs embrace technological change. We'll explore the psychological factors that enable adaptability to

evolving technology.

2. Innovation through Technology: Technology is a catalyst for innovation. We'll discuss how entrepreneurs leverage technology to create novel products, services, and business models.

Digital Transformation

1. Digital Strategy: Entrepreneurs must develop a comprehensive digital strategy. We'll delve into how the psychology of strategic thinking guides entrepreneurs in adopting and implementing technology.

2. Data-Driven Decision-Making: Data analytics is a valuable tool for entrepreneurial decision-making. We'll explore the psychological aspects of leveraging data for insights and informed choices.

Embracing E-Commerce

1. E-Commerce Strategies: The digital realm offers vast opportunities for e-commerce. We'll discuss how entrepreneurs create effective e-commerce strategies and the psychological principles behind these strategies.

2. Digital Marketing: Entrepreneurs use digital marketing to reach and engage customers. We'll explore the psychology of effective digital marketing, from social media to content creation.

Technology and Innovation

1. Open Innovation: Collaborative innovation is a hallmark of the digital age. We'll discuss how entrepreneurs engage in open innovation and foster creative partnerships.

2. Disruptive Technologies: Disruptive technologies challenge the status

quo. We'll explore how entrepreneurs embrace and harness disruptive technologies to reshape industries.

Challenges of Technology Integration

1. Cybersecurity and Privacy: Entrepreneurs must navigate the complex landscape of cybersecurity and privacy. We'll discuss the psychological aspects of safeguarding digital assets and customer information.

2. Digital Overload: The constant influx of digital information can be overwhelming. We'll explore how entrepreneurs manage digital overload and maintain a healthy work-life balance.

Case Studies and Real-Life Experiences

Throughout this chapter, we will draw on the experiences of successful entrepreneurs who have effectively integrated technology into their ventures. These real-life case studies will illustrate the psychological principles discussed and provide practical examples of how entrepreneurs have leveraged technology for business success.

Practical Exercises

To help you apply the concepts explored in this chapter, practical exercises and technology integration scenarios are included. These exercises are designed to guide you in developing the psychological skills and mindset needed to navigate the digital frontier in your own entrepreneurial endeavors.

Conclusion

Chapter 8 illuminates the crucial role of technology in entrepreneurship, emphasizing the need for entrepreneurs to embrace digital innovation and adapt to the ever-changing technological landscape. Entrepreneurs who understand the psychological dimensions of technology integration can harness its potential for growth, efficiency, and innovation, positioning their ventures for success in the digital age. In the next chapter, we will explore the role of leadership in entrepreneurship, highlighting the attributes and strategies that make for effective entrepreneurial leadership.

9

Entrepreneurial Leadership: Guiding Vision to Reality

Introduction

Entrepreneurial success often hinges on effective leadership. In Chapter 9, we dive into the vital role of leadership in entrepreneurship, exploring the psychological dimensions of what it takes to guide vision into reality. This chapter provides insights into the mindset and attributes of successful entrepreneurial leaders and offers guidance on how aspiring entrepreneurs can develop and refine their leadership skills.

Entrepreneurial leadership is not merely about directing a business; it's about inspiring teams, fostering innovation, and navigating the complex challenges of the entrepreneurial journey. Understanding the psychological foundations of leadership is essential for entrepreneurs seeking to create thriving and dynamic organizations.

The Entrepreneurial Leadership Mindset

1. Visionary Thinking: Entrepreneurial leaders are visionary thinkers. We'll discuss the psychological aspects of creating and communicating a compelling vision that inspires others.

2. Resilience and Adaptability: The entrepreneurial journey is rife with challenges. We'll explore the psychological traits that enable leaders to remain resilient and adaptable in the face of adversity.

Building High-Performing Teams

1. Team Dynamics: Effective leadership is about understanding and managing team dynamics. We'll discuss the psychological principles of teamwork, collaboration, and conflict resolution.

2. Motivation and Engagement: Entrepreneurs must motivate and engage their teams. We'll explore the psychology of intrinsic and extrinsic motivation and how to keep employees engaged.

Leading with Emotional Intelligence

1. Emotional Intelligence: Emotional intelligence is a critical attribute for entrepreneurial leaders. We'll delve into the psychological dimensions of emotional intelligence, including self-awareness, empathy, and relationship management.

2. Conflict Resolution: Conflicts are inevitable in any organization. We'll explore how leaders use emotional intelligence to navigate and resolve conflicts effectively.

Strategies for Effective Leadership

1. Delegation and Empowerment: Effective leaders delegate authority and empower their teams. We'll discuss the psychology of delegation and how to

create a culture of empowerment.

2. Communication and Feedback: Communication is a cornerstone of leadership. We'll explore the psychological aspects of effective communication, including active listening and providing constructive feedback.

Ethical Leadership

1. Ethical Decision-Making: Ethical leadership is about making principled decisions. We'll discuss the psychological principles behind ethical leadership and the role of values and integrity.

2. Corporate Social Responsibility: Entrepreneurs lead by example in corporate social responsibility. We'll explore how ethical leaders integrate social responsibility into their organizations.

Case Studies and Real-Life Experiences

Throughout this chapter, we will draw on the experiences of successful entrepreneurial leaders who have demonstrated exceptional leadership in their ventures. These real-life case studies will illustrate the psychological principles discussed and provide practical examples of how entrepreneurial leaders have guided their organizations to success.

Practical Exercises

To help you apply the concepts explored in this chapter, practical exercises and leadership scenarios are included. These exercises are designed to guide you in developing the psychological skills and mindset needed to become an effective entrepreneurial leader in your own endeavors.

Conclusion

Chapter 9 emphasizes the pivotal role of leadership in entrepreneurship, highlighting the attributes, strategies, and psychological principles that underpin effective leadership in the entrepreneurial context. Entrepreneurs who understand and apply these principles can inspire and guide their teams, foster innovation, and navigate the complexities of the entrepreneurial journey, ultimately realizing their vision and achieving success. In the final chapter, we will bring together the key insights and lessons from this book, providing a roadmap for aspiring and current entrepreneurs to thrive in the world of entrepreneurship.

10

Thriving in Entrepreneurship: A Roadmap to Success

Introduction

In this final chapter, we bring together the key insights and lessons from this book to provide a comprehensive roadmap for thriving in the world of entrepreneurship. We have explored the psychology of entrepreneurship, from understanding the entrepreneurial mindset to decision-making, resilience, creativity, ethics, technology, and leadership. Now, it's time to synthesize these insights into a practical guide that aspiring and current entrepreneurs can use to navigate their entrepreneurial journeys.

Thriving in entrepreneurship is not just about financial success but also about personal fulfillment, making a positive impact, and leaving a legacy. In this chapter, we offer a roadmap that encompasses both the foundational principles and the advanced strategies that can guide you on your entrepreneurial path.

The Entrepreneur's Roadmap

THE PSYCHOLOGY OF ENTREPRENEURSHIP: UNDERSTANDING THE MIND OF SUCCESS

1. Understanding the Entrepreneurial Mindset: We begin by emphasizing the importance of cultivating the entrepreneurial mindset, encompassing motivation, risk tolerance, resilience, creativity, and ethical values. This is the foundation upon which your entrepreneurial journey is built.

2. The Journey Begins: From Idea to Action: Start by recognizing and refining your entrepreneurial ideas, setting clear goals, and overcoming the fear of taking action. Develop a plan and take the leap into entrepreneurship.

3. Navigating Business Development and Growth: As your venture progresses, you'll need to shift your focus to business development and growth. Maintain a clear vision, engage in strategic thinking, and employ creativity and innovation to set your business apart.

4. Mastering Decision-Making: Decision-making is an ongoing challenge in entrepreneurship. Apply the cognitive and emotional strategies we've discussed to make informed choices and adapt to the ever-changing landscape.

5. Resilience: Bouncing Back from Setbacks: Resilience is your secret weapon for enduring and thriving through the inevitable setbacks and challenges. Cultivate a resilience mindset, learn from failure, and manage stress effectively.

6. Ethics and Social Responsibility: Building a business that is ethical and socially responsible is not just good for society; it's good for business. Integrate ethical values into your organization, practice corporate social responsibility, and engage stakeholders responsibly.

7. Technology Integration: Leverage technology to enhance efficiency, reach a broader audience, and drive innovation. Embrace a technological mindset, create a digital strategy, and stay adaptable in the digital era.

8. Entrepreneurial Leadership: Effective leadership is the glue that holds your

organization together. Lead with a visionary mindset, foster high-performing teams, and practice ethical leadership.

9. The Art of Delegation: As your venture grows, delegation becomes crucial. Master the art of delegation and empower your team to achieve more.

10. Communication and Feedback: Effective communication and feedback mechanisms are the cornerstones of leadership. Learn how to communicate with impact, listen actively, and provide constructive feedback.

11. Building an Innovative Culture: Foster a culture of innovation within your organization by engaging in open innovation, embracing disruptive technologies, and creating a creative and forward-thinking environment.

12. The Ethical Entrepreneur's Journey: Reflect on your journey as an ethical entrepreneur. Make principled decisions, prioritize corporate social responsibility, and lead by example.

13. The Digital Frontier: Navigating the digital frontier is an ongoing process. Stay technologically adaptable, develop a digital strategy, and leverage data-driven insights to guide your decisions.

14. Staying Resilient in Leadership: Just as resilience is crucial for entrepreneurs, it's essential for leaders. Develop a resilient leadership mindset, understand team dynamics, and maintain your emotional intelligence.

15. The Entrepreneur's Legacy: In the final step, consider the legacy you want to leave as an entrepreneur. Evaluate your impact on society, and strive to create a positive and enduring legacy.

Conclusion

The journey of entrepreneurship is multifaceted, challenging, and rewarding.

This roadmap is designed to provide you with a structured and comprehensive guide to navigate this journey, whether you are just starting out or seeking to refine your entrepreneurial skills. By understanding and applying the psychological principles, strategies, and mindsets discussed throughout this book, you can thrive in entrepreneurship, realize your vision, and leave a lasting legacy in the world of business.

11

Summary

Chapter 1: The Psychology of Entrepreneurship: Understanding the Mind of Success
- Introduction to the psychology of entrepreneurship.
- Exploring the entrepreneurial mindset.
- Key psychological traits and characteristics of successful entrepreneurs.

Chapter 2: The Entrepreneurial Journey: From Idea to Action
- Starting the entrepreneurial journey with inspiration and passion.
- Idea validation, risk-taking, and goal-setting.
- Proactive behavior and adaptability.

Chapter 3: Business Development and Growth: Navigating the Entrepreneurial Landscape
- Clarifying the vision and strategic thinking.
- Leadership and team building for business growth.
- Financial management, market expansion, and competition.

Chapter 4: Entrepreneurial Decision-Making: Navigating Uncertainty and Complexity
- Cognitive biases, emotions, and risk assessment in decision-making.
- Strategic and operational decision-making.

- Collaborative decision-making and delegation.

Chapter 5: Resilience: The Entrepreneur's Secret Weapon
  - The resilience mindset and strategies.
  - Coping with failure, handling setbacks, and managing stress.
  - Case studies and practical exercises on building resilience.

Chapter 6: Creativity and Innovation: The Entrepreneur's Competitive Edge
  - Understanding the creative mindset and divergent thinking.
  - Problem-solving strategies and fostering innovation.
  - Case studies and practical exercises on creativity and innovation.

Chapter 7: Ethics and Social Responsibility in Entrepreneurship
  - Ethical decision-making and moral values.
  - Building ethical ventures, corporate social responsibility, and sustainability.
  - Case studies and practical exercises on ethical entrepreneurship.

Chapter 8: Technology and Entrepreneurship: Navigating the Digital Frontier
  - Technological adaptability and innovation through technology.
  - Digital transformation, e-commerce, and digital marketing.
  - Challenges and opportunities in technology integration.

Chapter 9: Entrepreneurial Leadership: Guiding Vision to Reality
  - Visionary thinking, resilience, and adaptability in leadership.
  - Building high-performing teams, leading with emotional intelligence.
  - Ethical leadership and effective leadership strategies.

Chapter 10: Thriving in Entrepreneurship: A Roadmap to Success
  - A comprehensive roadmap for entrepreneurship, encompassing key concepts and strategies.
  - Covering the entrepreneurial mindset, decision-making, resilience, ethics,

SUMMARY

technology, and leadership.

- Fostering a fulfilling, impactful, and legacy-driven entrepreneurial journey.

These chapters provide a comprehensive guide to understanding the psychology of entrepreneurship and offer practical insights and exercises to help aspiring and current entrepreneurs succeed in the complex and dynamic world of business.

12

Chapter 12

www.ingramcontent.com/pod-product-compliance
Lightning Source LLC
LaVergne TN
LVHW021054100526
838202LV00083B/5949